This collection of images was produced by local artist Joseph A. Mulac and is part of a series of watercolors depicting various scenes in the community. This particular piece includes sites and landmarks in the South Chicago community.

IMAGES
of America

CHICAGO'S
SOUTHEAST SIDE

Revisited

IMAGES
of America

CHICAGO'S
SOUTHEAST SIDE

Revisited

Rod Sellers

ARCADIA
PUBLISHING

Published by Arcadia Publishing
Charleston, South Carolina

Library of Congress Catalog Card Number: 2001093318

For all general information contact Arcadia Publishing at:
Telephone 843-853-2070
Fax 843-853-0044
E-mail sales@arcadiapublishing.com
For customer service and orders:
Toll-Free 1-888-313-2665

Visit us on the Internet at www.arcadiapublishing.com

An early postcard from 1910 contains several "Views From South Chicago."

CONTENTS

A second set of images from artist Joseph Mulac depicts locations and landmarks in the East Side community. These paintings were commissioned by the Royal Savings and Loan Association to commemorate their 100th anniversary in 1987.

INTRODUCTION

The story of Southeast Chicago is one that illustrates major themes of American urban history. One theme is diversity: ecological diversity and the ongoing conflict between man and nature, and ethnic, religious, and cultural diversity which resulted as immigrant groups poured into this industrial area in search of jobs. After the Civil War, common urban-American themes included industrialization, urbanization, immigration, unionization, and Americanization. All these themes are present in the history of the Southeast Side.

When the Ice Age ended, Chicago's Southeast Side was covered by the waters of Lake Chicago, the predecessor to Lake Michigan. Over thousands of years, the Lake receded, and the landscape of the region emerged. Marshes, prairies, beaches, ponds, small lakes, and wandering shallow rivers remained. An abundance of plant and animal life thrived.

The area was originally a frontier region where hunting, trapping, and fishing were the main activities. Native Americans and, subsequently, Europeans engaged in these pursuits initially as a means of survival and later as a form of recreation. When South Chicago began to develop in 1836, it was the era of canal building. The original South Chicago speculator, Lewis Benton, bought land along the Calumet River and built the Calumet House, a stagecoach stop, and the Eagle Hotel in what was then called the City of Calumet. He did this with hopes that a canal connecting the Saint Lawrence River and Great Lakes water system with the Mississippi River system would be built in the Calumet Region. It was, but not until the 1920s. The construction of the Illinois Michigan Canal and the Depression of 1837 temporarily postponed area development. The Southeast Side lay dormant until the railroads arrived in the area.

With the coming of the railroads in 1848, the City of Calumet was renamed Ainsworth, the name of the railroad station. South Deering dates its origins to 1845. The East Side came into being in 1851 when a Potawatomi Native American woman named Togah sold a section of land near present day Calumet Park to George W. Ewing. More and more railroads laid their tracks through the area and created the foundation for a post-Civil War boom that would draw industry and people to the region.

The improvement of the Calumet River was the key to the industrial development of the Southeast Side and the drawing card that brought large numbers of residents, mostly immigrants, to the area seeking the jobs in local factories. James H. Bowen and other investors founded the Calumet and Chicago Canal and Dock Company in 1869. Congress appropriated funds for improvements in the Calumet River, and in 1873 South Chicago was made a port of entry. In 1874, 6,000 acres of land were platted for a new town where Benton had purchased land earlier. The river was deepened and docks, piers, bridges, and other improvements were made.

Perhaps the most important event of local history was the opening of the Joseph H. Brown Iron and Steel Company rolling mill (later named Wisconsin Steel) at 109th and the Calumet River in 1875. This proved that the Calumet River was navigable, and industrial expansion occurred rapidly. North Chicago Rolling Mill (later named United States Steel) opened a steel mill at the mouth of the Calumet River in 1880. Numerous other industrial businesses came to the area, mostly locating along the Calumet River or on Lake Michigan.

This was the boom period for the communities of the Southeast Side. South Chicago, South Deering, the East Side, and Hegewisch grew as newcomers were drawn to the area by both the numerous jobs available in heavy industry as well as the jobs necessary to support the growing population of the area. The immigration patterns on the Southeast Side mirrored those of the country as a whole. The Northern and Western European English, Welsh, and Scotch were followed by Irish, Germans, and Swedes. They, in turn, were followed by Southern and Eastern Europeans in the latter part of the nineteenth and early part of the twentieth centuries, when Polish, Lithuanian, Slovenian, Slovakian, Croatian, Serbian, Italian, Greek, and Hungarian immigrants, Eastern European Jews, and others became Southeast Siders. During and after World War I, with the decline in European immigration and the immigration quotas of the 1920s, African Americans and Mexicans began to enter the area. In recent years, Puerto Ricans, Arabs, Haitians, Ethiopians, and others have made their homes in Southeast Chicago. At present, the Mexican population is the fastest growing group in the area. These immigration patterns are most obvious in the formation of neighborhood churches, ethnic organizations, and institutions.

As the communities grew, problems arose. Fire was a constant threat in communities that were not subject to some of the construction restrictions that Chicago imposed after the 1871 Chicago Fire. The Southeast Side, originally part of the Village of Hyde Park, did not become part of Chicago until 1889. Wooden two-flats and three-flats were always in danger from fire, and there were several serious church fires: Immaculate Conception, Bethlehem Lutheran, Saint Francis De Sales, and Saint Patrick's were all victims, and terrible fires occurred in the grain elevators along the Calumet River. The residents of the Southeast Side also dealt with the same problems that other Americans faced. The Great Depression hit the area hard; community residents lost jobs or worked shortened hours, some lost their homes, and businesses and banks closed. The Depression years were followed by World War II. Community residents served in the Armed Forces, and many gave their lives for their country. In addition, the "Home Front" contributed to the war effort in many ways: production in area factories increased, producing war materials in great quantities. Even children participated in scrap drives, victory gardens, and paper drives. Labor unions were also important organizations in the community, and from time to time, there were strikes and other labor difficulties. In recent years, the community has faced environmental concerns and damage caused by heavy industry; the area has a proliferation of land fills and waste sites, which has led to a strong grass roots environmental movement. Beginning with the closing of Wisconsin Steel in 1980, thousands of area residents lost their jobs as the American steel industry went through a serious decline. In 1990, there was an attempt to replace much of the area with the Lake Calumet Airport. Area residents vigorously opposed the airport, and the plan died.

What does the future hold for the Southeast Side? There is a need for economic development and jobs but not at the expense of the environment. The region has the largest quantity of vacant land in the city of Chicago. It also has some of the best natural and wetland areas, although many are in need of remediation. Some signs are positive. Solo Cup has purchased part of the vacant U.S. Steel property for expansion; Ford Motor Company has plans for a supplier park near its plant; the National Park Service has proposed creating a Calumet National Heritage Area which would include the Southeast Side; and the City of Chicago has plans to build an Environmental Center for the area. Thus, the tension between development and natural preservation continues today as it has existed in the past.

One

THE EARLY YEARS

SOUTH CHICAGO IN 1870.

The natural landscape of the Southeast Side or Calumet region was greatly altered by the coming of industry. The earliest changes occurred as the first railroads were built to pass through the area on their way to Chicago. The railroads were built on Native American trails, which followed the sand ridges that separated various marshes and wetlands. Railroads first entered the region in the late 1840s. Early industrial development on the Southeast Side occurred after the Civil War and was concentrated around the Calumet River, "Chicago's Other River." The river's connection to Lake Michigan and its potential to transport the heavy bulk materials needed in the making of steel was the focal point of industrial development in the region. However, before development could take place, numerous changes needed to be made in the shallow, meandering prairie river. At the mouth of the Calumet River, shown here in 1870, a large sand bar (similar to the sand bar originally located at the mouth of the Chicago River) created a bend in the river just before it emptied into Lake Michigan. The Calumet River would have to be widened, deepened, and straightened, and a channel would have to be cut through the sand bar before the river could be used profitably.

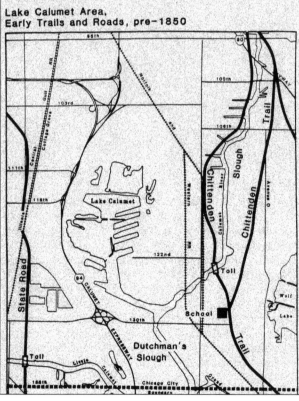

Lake Calumet Area,
Early Trails and Roads, pre-1850

Before settlers ever came to the area, Native Americans passed through the area using numerous trails. There were villages near 79th and Lake Michigan, on the north side of Lake Calumet, and on the south side of Wolf Lake. This painting, one of four murals on the second floor of the Calumet Park Field House, was painted by artist Tom Lea in 1928 and reflects the artist's interpretation of early life on the Southeast Side.

This map shows some early roads that passed through the area prior to 1850. The earliest roads ran along the Lake Michigan shoreline. In 1847, the Chittenden Road provided a transportation route east of Lake Calumet. (Map courtesy of Dr. James E. Landing and University of Illinois at Chicago, Department of Geography Cartography Laboratory.)

The first railroad through the Southeast Side was the Lake Shore and Michigan Southern. It arrived in 1848 along the lakefront and passed through the East Side, South Chicago, and then to Englewood on its way to downtown Chicago. In 1857, a train station was opened and named Ainsworth, one of the early names used for the community. This is a more recent view of the train station located at approximately 94th and South Chicago Avenue.

The Lake Shore and Michigan Southern Railroad later became the New York Central. The Pennsylvania and Fort Wayne, and Elgin and Eastern and Joliet (EJ&E) soon followed. In 1873, a train station originally named Colehour was opened at 100th Street and Ewing Avenue. The railroad tracks, which paralleled Indianapolis Boulevard, also divided the East Side into the Taylorville section north of the tracks and the Colehour section south of the tracks. Pictured is the East Side Station, May 1909.

Another important railroad in the region was the Illinois Central. It created a branch line to South Chicago in 1883. Pictured are workers for the Illinois Central at 118th and Torrence, near the Cargill Grain Elevator in 1926.

Hegewisch was the last of the four Southeast Side communities to develop because of its location between the railroads that ran along the lakefront and those to the west near Lake Calumet. In the 1880s, the railroads finally arrived and Hegewisch's development began. The picture above shows railroad tracks that ran through the eastern portion of Hegewisch commonly referred to as "Arizona" because of the sandy landscape and the varieties of plant life that grew in the area.

The Chicago & Western Indiana and Pennsylvania railroads opened Hegewisch stations in the 1880s. Pictured is the Pennsylvania Railroad station at 134th and Mackinaw Avenue. It was the location of the first train to carry passengers from Hegewisch.

Many industries developed because of the railroads. The Ryan Car Company was located in Hegewisch. The company rebuilt railroad cars. This is a photo of a rail junction near the company.

The Elgin, Joliet, and Eastern Railway, also known as the Chicago Outer Belt Line, was a line that linked cities and towns located on other railroad lines radiating out from the city of Chicago like spokes of a bicycle. It connected United States Steel plants located in Joliet, Gary, and South Chicago. Pictured is a steam locomotive of the EJ&E railroad, c.1920.

Transportation within the communities was initially provided by horse cars that ran along Commercial Avenue from 87th Street to 92nd Street and then to the East Side to 106th and Ewing Avenue. They began service in 1884. They were soon replaced by numerous trolley lines. This is an early trolley at 101st and Ewing Avenue c. 1890.

James H. Bowen was the president of the Calumet and Chicago Canal and Dock Company. The company was founded in 1869 by a group of investors who were largely responsible for the early industrial development of the Southeast Side. Bowen is often referred to as the "Father of South Chicago." Bowen described South Chicago in 1870 as follows: "There were a few small dwellings occupied by fishers, hunters, and workers in nuisances. No roads were there that could be traversed. No improvements in the mouth of the river . . . no offices, no churches or school buildings . . . "

Chicago. Ill. Factory district in South Chicago.

The Calumet and Chicago Canal and Dock Company successfully lobbied Congress for legislation that provided funds to deepen the river and improve other facilities. In 1873, South Chicago was made a port of entry. Early development, as seen in this post card view, was concentrated along the river.

15

BIRDSEYE VIEW OF SOUTH CHICAGO CALUMET HARBOR.

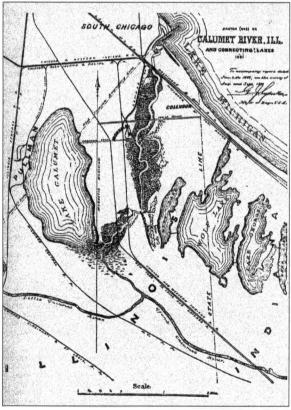

In 1874, the company subdivided 6,000 acres of land and began the sale of property in what later became South Chicago. This view shows the changes already made in the river and the early industrial development in the region. The smoke in the picture was not considered to be a negative feature; in fact, it was a sign of prosperity and an indication of the jobs to be had in the numerous factories and businesses of the Southeast Side.

This 1881 Army Corps of Engineers map depicts some of the shallow lakes of the Calumet region (from left to right: Lake Calumet, Hyde Lake, Wolf Lake, Lake George, and Deer Lake), which have since been altered by development. Much of Lake Calumet has been filled in, and many of the extensive wetlands, which stretched to the Calumet River, have been eliminated. Hyde Lake and Deer Lake have been filled in for development and are gone.

16

According to the stationary of the Knickerbocker Ice Company, headquartered in downtown Chicago, the largest icehouses in the world were located on Wolf Lake. Phil Schmidt, founder of a well-known restaurant in the Calumet region, worked for the company cutting ice when he was a young man. This scene shows workers harvesting ice on Wolf Lake.

This early 1900s view of the Calumet River looks southeast toward Ewing Avenue and the 92nd Street bridge. The railroad tracks in the left part of the picture are the EJ&E Railroad, which crossed the Calumet River and entered U.S. Steel. To the right of center is the steeple of Saint George's church.

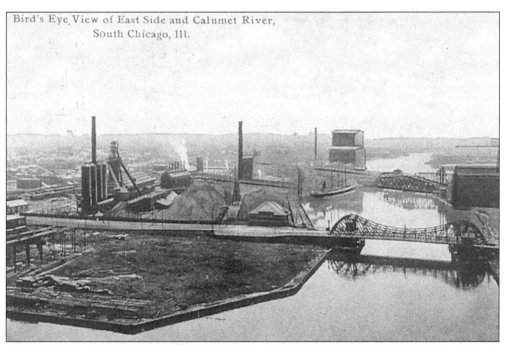

An early 1900s post card view of the mouth of the Calumet River shows the changes in the configuration of the shoreline after the sand bar had been eliminated and the river entrance widened. On the "East Side" of the river are the smokestacks of Iroquois Steel, and further down the river, beyond the 92nd and 95th Street bridges, is a grain elevator.

Every Southeast Sider has undergone the inconvenience of being stopped by a bridge or by a train. This post card view of the 95th Street Bridge depicts a common occurrence that has been a part of daily life for area residents for a long time.

18

The Calumet River has never been known for its aesthetic value. It was a working river, and most traffic on the river was commercial or industrial, as shown in this post card view of the Calumet River at 102nd Street.

An ore boat, heading south, passes under the railroad bridges that cross the Calumet River at about 96th Street. The heavy bulk materials used to make steel, which included iron ore, coal, and limestone, were transported most economically by ship. Several steel mills were therefore located on the banks of the Calumet River.

In 1958, the Chicago Skyway was built linking the Indiana Toll Road with Chicago. Initially, the toll was 25¢, and it has increased steadily to the current $2 toll for the eight-mile roadway. This view shows the Skyway reaching across the Calumet River as construction nears completion.

With the completion of the expanded St. Lawrence Seaway in 1959, Chicago had the capability of handling increased amounts of ocean-going shipping. Lake Calumet Harbor, shown here, represents the inland terminus of the Seaway. However, barge traffic continues inland on the Illinois Waterway up the Calumet River system to the Cal Sag channel and eventually to the Mississippi River.

Two

INDUSTRIAL

DEVELOPMENT

The story of Chicago's Southeast Side is the story of steel. At one point, the region was one of the largest steel producing regions in the world. Heavy industry, especially steel mills, came to the area after the Civil War, drawn by natural features compatible with their business. There was cheap land and plenty of it—land that would be used for factories, bulk storage, and disposal. Fresh water was present—water for cooling, necessary in the manufacturing process, and water for transportation. Railroads had already crossed the area and linked the Southeast Side to other regions of the country. There was an available supply of labor and space for housing more workers. The region was far enough from Chicago to minimize the negative features of heavy industry on the city yet close enough to take advantage of the markets of the Chicago metropolitan region.

The largest employer on the Southeast Side was United States Steel. At its peak, the plant had about 18,000 workers. This picture shows the employment office at the mill, which was then named Illinois Steel Company.

The Joseph H. Brown Iron and Steel Company began construction of the first major steel mill on Chicago's Southeast Side in July 1875. The mill was located on the west bank of the Calumet River at 109th Street. The first ore boat, the *J.L. Hurd*, carefully made its way up the river and unloaded its cargo of iron ore. After several ownership and name changes, the operation became known as Wisconsin Steel in 1902 when International Harvester gained control of the mill.

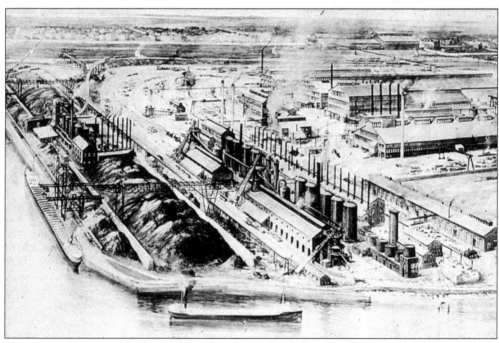

The early mill consisted of a rolling mill and a nail mill. It normally employed 1,000 to 1,500 workers, most of whom lived near the mill in rooming houses along Torrence Avenue. The following activities took place on the site: coke production, pig iron production, steel making, casting and primary rolling, and blooming and manufacturing millwork. Pictured is an aerial view of the plant facing west.

At one time, Wisconsin Steel employed 5,000 workers. This 1934 picture shows employees of the coke plant who had been employed for more than ten years. The men seated on the bench had been employed by the company for more than fifteen years.

Area mills provided some social services for their employees. The Goodfellows Club from Wisconsin Steel gave workers an opportunity to recreate and socialize. The club also provided community service. Here a wagon-load of Christmas gifts for the needy awaits delivery *c.* 1918.

This is a view of the machine shop at Wisconsin Steel *c.* 1921. Workers in the machine shop were responsible for maintenance and repair of all the steel-making equipment in the mill.

Much of the land in the Calumet region was wetland, so it was cheap. It provided a place to dump slag, the refuse from the steel-making process. After the molten slag cooled and hardened, it was used as fill to reclaim many low-lying areas. The neighborhood north of the mill was known as Slag Valley. Residents and visitors often watched the slag dumping as a form of visual recreation.

Shown are four elements crucial to understanding the history of this steel-producing community: the worker, the mill (United States Steel South Works), the church (St. Michael Archangel Catholic Church), and the houses of the Bush neighborhood. These elements reflect key symbols of Southeast Chicago.

This early post card view shows Illinois Steel Company's harbor with early buildings of South Chicago in the background. The picture was taken in the early 1900s. Illinois Steel Company later developed into United States Steel Corporation.

When North Chicago Rolling Mill, the predecessor to U.S. Steel South Works, came to the Southeast Side in 1880, they started with 73 acres of land. Their property had 1,500 feet of frontage on the Calumet River and 2,500 feet on Lake Michigan. Slag from the steel-making process was dumped in a lake front area, increasing the land area for future expansion. This picture shows the furthest extent of the mill, which eventually covered over 570 acres.

DANGER

KEEP AWAY FROM VESSELS WHEN FIRST HEAT IS BLOWING ON A NEW BOTTOM ALSO WHEN BELL RINGS AS VESSEL IS BEING SCRAPPED.

ORZ STE SA DALEKO OD VESSELA, KEOJ PRVA HITZA SA BLOVUJE NA NOVEM SPODKU, I KEDJ ZVONI, LEBO VTEM CASE SZA SCRAP HADZE OO VESSELA.

TARTSATOK MAGATOKAT TAVOL OLYAN MEDENCZETOL (VESSEL), MELY AZ ELSÖ HOSEGET FUJJA UJ FENEKEN, ES HA CSENGETNEK, MERT AKKOR A SCREPPET DOBJAK BE A VESZLIBA.

DRŽI SE DALEKO OD VESELA KAD PRVI ŽAR ZAPIRI NA NOVO TLO; TAKODJER PAZI KAD ZVONO ZAZVONI, JER JE TO ZNAK DA SE VESEL SKRAPUJE.

TRZYMAJ SIĘ ZDALA OD ZBIORNIKA KIEDY PIERWSZE GORĄCO IDZIE NA SPÓD I STUCHAJ NA DZWONKI, BO ZBIORNIKI BEDA "SKEPOWANE."

GENERAL SUPERINTENDENT

In about 1900, Illinois Steel South Works employed about 6,000 people. Almost one-fourth of them did not speak English, so signs needed to be made in multiple languages. The above warning sign is in five languages. The largest ethnic group employed at the mill at this time was Polish.

This photo depicts the scene that occurs as molten steel is being poured. It is beautiful but dangerous, and it reflects the danger inherent in working in a steel mill. Accidents in the mills were common and often serious.

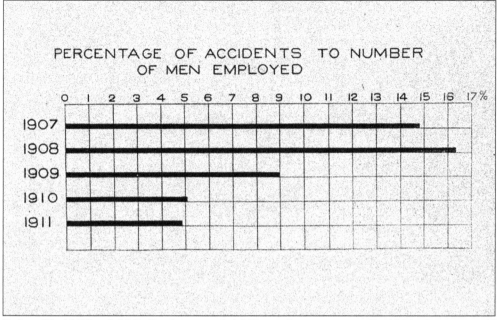

PERCENTAGE OF ACCIDENTS TO NUMBER
OF MEN EMPLOYED

Before World War I, U.S. Steel averaged 1,200 accidents per year. In 1906, there were 46 fatalities, and 41 of those were in separate accidents. The company began a safety program that reduced the number of accidents. This graph shows a reduction in accidents at South Works during the years 1907–1911. Even this reduced accident rate would be unacceptable by today's standards.

This 1937 photo shows that the plant safety program had achieved some measure of success. However, mills were still very dangerous places to work. Safety campaigns were a frequent occurrence in the mill.

A variety of steel-making methods were used at South Works. Initially, blast furnaces and Bessemer converters were used. Later the open-hearth furnaces, as pictured to the right, were used. They were considered to be more efficient than blast furnaces. The first use of an open hearth at South Works was February 11, 1895. It took about seven hours to make steel in an open-hearth furnace.

South Works had its own fire department (shown here), police force, hospital clinic, and ambulance service. It was, in effect, a self-contained city. There was even an electrical power-generating station on the property. This generating station is one of only a few remaining buildings left standing on the property at the time of this book's publication.

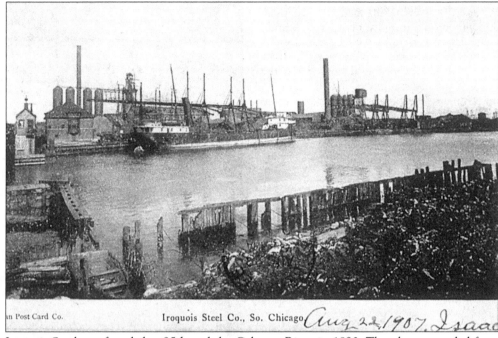

Iroquois Steel Co., So. Chicago *Aug 22/1907. Isaac*

Iroquois Steel was founded at 95th and the Calumet River in 1890. The plant extended from the lake to the E.J. & E. railroad tracks on the Calumet River's east side. Ships were unloaded at an ore dock rather than pulling into a slip, as seen in this photo. Electric unloading machines were capable of unloading a 10,000-ton ship within 10 to 12 hours.

In 1923, Youngstown Sheet and Tube Company took over what was formerly Iroquois Steel. The name comes from a neighborhood legend, which stated that a Native-American burial ground was located there at the mouth of the Calumet River. There was a cemetery used by early settlers at this location. It was used until about 1860.

30

Grand Crossing Tack Company was located at 79th and South Chicago Avenue until the company moved to the East Side in 1901. They purchased a site at 118th and the Calumet River and built two open-hearth furnaces and a 35-inch blooming mill. During World War II, the government built several steel-making facilities that were operated by Republic Steel. After the war, the company purchased those facilities from the government. The above view shows the early mill in a wetland area of Hyde Lake.

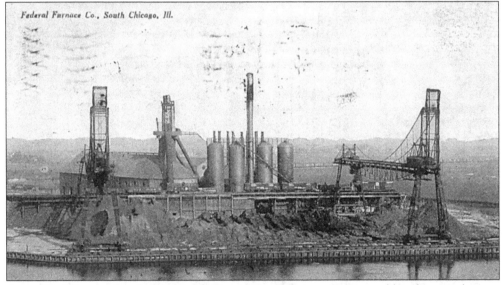

Acme Steel has a coke plant in South Deering on Torrence Avenue, a blast furnace plant on the East Side along the Calumet River, and a finishing mill in Riverdale, a nearby suburb. It is the last remaining integrated steel maker in the region. By Products Coke Corporation built the coke plant in 1905, and purchased Federal Furnace, pictured here, in 1915. In 1929, the company became Interlake Iron Corporation. In December 1964, Acme Steel and Interlake Iron Company merged to form Interlake Steel Corporation. Acme Steel was a spin-off of Interlake in 1986.

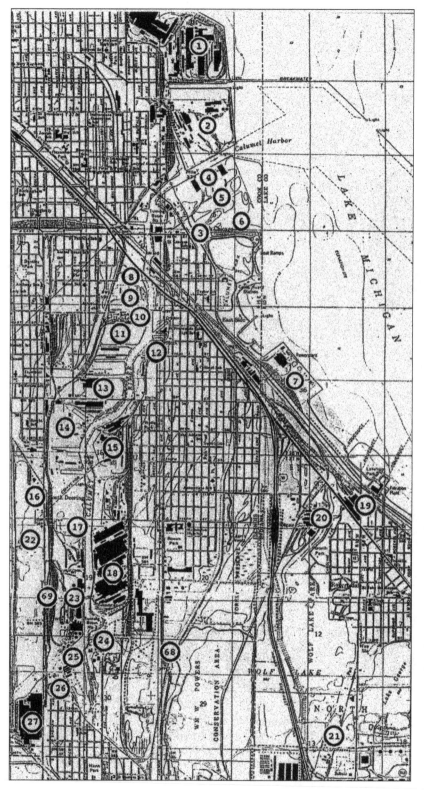

This map, prepared by Keith Ryder of the Army Corps of Engineers, shows major industries located on Chicago's Southeast Side. Most are on the Calumet River. Among the industrial sites are (1 & 2) United States Steel; (5) Iroquois Steel, later Youngstown Steel; (13) General Mills; (14) Wisconsin Steel; (15) Interlake Iron and Steel; (16) By Products Coke Corporation; (18) Republic Steel; and (27) Ford Motor Company.

Each of the four Southeast Side communities had a major mill. Pressed Steel, shown above, was located in Hegewisch, south of Brainard Avenue. It was the successor of U.S. Rolling Stock Company, founded by A. Hegewisch in 1883. Western Steel and foundry was a successor.

There were many factories and plants other than steel mills on the Southeast Side. Pictured are the State Line Generating Station of Commonwealth Edison and the Albert Schwill Company later owned by the Falstaff Brewing Company. The State Line Generating Station is built on landfill and is actually located in the state of Indiana.

In 1902, the Wabash Railroad built the Rialto Elevator on a slip of the Calumet River at 104th Street. A year later, the Star and Crescent Milling Company built a flour mill on the other side of the slip. A cereal plant was built on the site in 1923, and all were combined in 1929 with the formation of General Mills. Among the products produced at the South Chicago plant were Gold Medal Cake Flour, Wheaties, Bisquick, Kix, Cheerios, Betty Crocker Soup, Betty Crocker Cake Mixes, Cocoa Puffs, Trix, and others. The plant closed in 1995.

Access to the Calumet River made shipyards an obvious industry for the Southeast Side. Several businesses, like the Chicago Shipbuilding Company shown above, developed to build ships or to repair them. Rooming houses, taverns, and restaurants in the community also benefited from ships that came to the area.

An early East Side company, founded by Martin Hausler, merged with Great Lakes Dredge and Dock Company in 1903. The company accomplished numerous water front improvements. Pictured is diver William Lehndorf, assisted by Fred Blank Sr., preparing to enter the water.

Great Lakes Dredge and Dock Company handled the job of preparing and transporting the captured World War II German submarine *U-505* to the Museum of Science and Industry in Chicago. This view shows the submarine at the company's 92nd street facility. A floating dry dock is submerged beneath the ship. The submarine would then be raised out of the water for repairs and transport. The 92nd Street Bridge over the Calumet River is in the background.

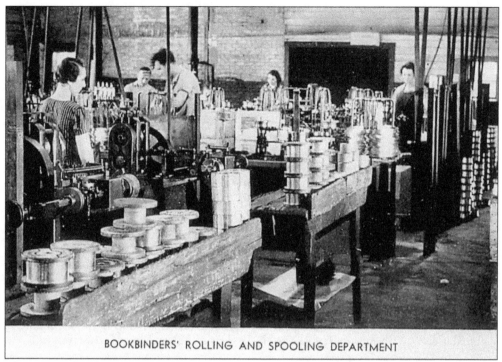

BOOKBINDERS' ROLLING AND SPOOLING DEPARTMENT

Chicago Steel and Wire Company was located at 103rd and Torrence Avenue and was founded in 1914. It was a finishing plant that used the steel produced in area mills to make wire and welding rods.

Ford has been making automobiles at its Chicago Assembly Plant since 1924. The plant, located near 130th and Torrence, originally built Model T's and then, in 1928, Model A's. During World War II, M-8 armored cars and M-20 reconnaissance armored units were built. Pictured is part of the Ford contribution to the war effort. In recent years, the Taurus and Sable cars have been produced at the area plant.

Three

SOUTH CHICAGO

Eighty-ninth and Muskegon Avenue — note absence of
paved streets and sidewalks. (Prior to 1910)

The thriving economy of area steel mills brought large numbers of residents into the area. The oldest of the Southeast Side communities was South Chicago. Although it dates its beginnings to 1836, the real development of South Chicago did not occur until heavy industry came to the region. Migrants and immigrants moved in and developed businesses, churches, schools, fraternal and social organizations, and a community where they could raise their children and support their families. South Chicago was the main "port of entry" for the Southeast Side. Once immigrants had become established and more financially secure, they often moved to the East Side or Hegewisch and, in later years, to the suburbs.

As people moved into the community seeking the jobs offered by local industry, housing was constructed to meet the demand. Most of the surrounding area was developed during the growth years of United States Steel South Works. Many lived in houses, two-flats, and apartments similar to these, pictured above, on the 8900 block of Muskegon Avenue.

37

The main shopping district in South Chicago was along Commercial Avenue from 93rd Street to 87th Street and along 92nd Street. Transfer points between various trolley and later bus lines made the district accessible, and businesses in the district thrived. This view shows one of the most important public transportation transfer points, the intersection of 92nd and Commercial Avenue.

Eighty-eight Street and Commercial Avenue —
Signs read, "Dever for Mayor."

By the 1920s, the shopping district was well developed. This view of 88th and Commercial shows a "Dever for Mayor" sign. William Dever ran against William Thompson for Mayor of Chicago in 1923. Down the block one can see Immaculate Conception Church, the first Polish-Catholic church in the area, founded in 1882.

Any product or necessity could be purchased on Commercial Avenue; there was no need to go to downtown Chicago. The Commercial Avenue shopping district also drew residents from neighboring communities who came to buy items not readily available in their neighborhood stores. This postcard view shows Commercial Avenue south from the five-and-ten store in the early 1900s.

An 1891 list of businesses in South Chicago along Commercial Avenue and along 92nd Street included 45 saloons, 40 clothing stores, 24 food stores, 9 hardware stores, 5 druggists, and numerous other businesses. This is a view of Commercial Avenue looking south from 87th Street.

By 1967, when this photo was taken, the business district continued to be very successful and, like the area steel mills, continued to fuel the local economy. In 1959, a 116-day extended steel strike caused much economic hardship in the community, not only for steelworkers but also for local businessmen. *The Daily Calumet* photographer Eugene Cichoracki took this picture with a special lens, which compressed a six-block stretch of Commercial from 93rd Street to 87th Street.

GOLDBLATT BROS. NEW STORE — 91st STREET and COMMERCIAL AVE.

Goldblatt's Department Store took over the building that formerly housed the Lederer Department Store. The old building was demolished, and when a new Goldblatt's building opened in December 1935, it was three stories tall, as shown in this post card view. Almost immediately, it was determined to be too small and by summer of 1936, plans were already being made to add two more stories to the building.

South Chicago Saving Bank was a very important financial institution in the community. On May 25, 1933, a parade was sponsored by the South Chicago Chamber of Commerce to celebrate the reopening of a newly decorated bank lobby. The bank opened in South Chicago in 1902 and moved into its 92nd Street and Commercial location in 1926.

This post card view from the early 1900s shows two important South Chicago landmarks: the Columbus Monument and the South Chicago Hotel. The Columbus Monument was a gift to the city of Chicago in 1892 from John B. Drake and was originally located near City Hall. In 1909, it was moved to the intersection of 92nd and Exchange. The South Chicago Hotel stood at the later location of the South Chicago Savings Bank.

This neoclassical structure served residents of South Chicago as their post office until it was torn down and removed. This beautiful building, which opened in 1913, is still missed by those who remember it. Its success proved to be its downfall. A lack of space for delivery trucks and for customer parking resulted in its being replaced by a new facility on 93rd and South Chicago Avenue.

Although it was not actually in the community of South Chicago, the South Chicago Hospital, now Trinity Hospital, has served that community since it was chartered by the state of Illinois in 1895. This post card shows the 1908 building that housed the hospital at that time.

Neighborhood theaters were a large part of the local people's lives. Every community had their own set of theaters. South Chicago at one time actually had eight theaters in walking distance of each other. As time progressed, these neighborhood theaters closed and moved to suburban shopping malls, and the last of the South Chicago movie theaters closed in the 1980s. Pictured is the Gayety Theater along with the candy and ice cream store of the same name.

The neighborhood newspaper of choice was *The Daily Calumet*. At its peak, its circulation area extended from 67th Street on the north to 138th Street on the south and from Stony Island on the west to Lake Michigan and the Indiana border on the east. The paper began publishing in 1881 as the *South Chicago Independent*. This photo shows the staff in front of the newspaper's office in 1910.

Social and civic groups were influential in building strong community ties. Lions Clubs, Masons, Civic Leagues, and Kiwanis Clubs were involved in numerous community service projects. Pictured are the South Chicago Kiwanis Club members in the mid-1960s as Paul Haller presents an award to Richard Snoddy.

Turn-of-the-century South Chicago police officer Curran provides special services to keep the crossing in front of the railroad station at 91st Street clear of snow.
The train station building later became Sonny's Restaurant, a well-known South Chicago eatery.

Most residents did their grocery shopping at small stores that were typically family owned and operated. Before modern refrigeration existed, most residents did their grocery shopping on an almost-daily basis at small nearby stores. The Colfax Grocery Store, pictured here, was located at 8400 S. Colfax. Pictured in this 1948 photo are Agnes Zielinski and her daughter Barbara.

The Johnson's Grocery Store was originally located at 8927 Superior, later named Burley Avenue. It opened in 1896. In 1911, the store moved to 8929 Burley. Customers were allowed to charge their purchases and pay their grocery bills on payday. Pictured from left are Mildred, John, Earl, and Lillie Johnson.

Many ethnic businesses developed to serve the tastes of various ethnic groups in the community. La Superior Tortillas was in business from 1939 until the owner closed it in 1960 due to illness. It was located at 3221 East 91st Street until 1952, and then moved to 9056 Brandon.

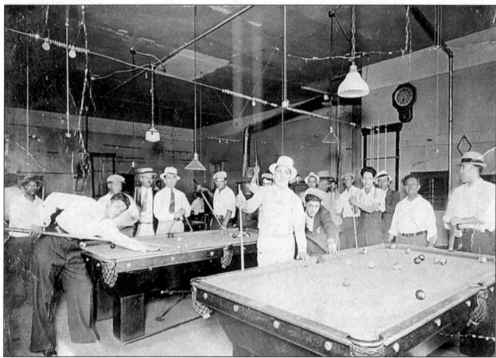

This pool hall provided recreational opportunities, primarily for young men of the area. It was located at 3221 East 91st Street after La Superior Tortillas moved to a different location.

Bars and saloons were numerous in the mill neighborhoods, and bartenders or saloon keepers were popular figures. Pictured is John "The Swede" Czaplewski in his bar at 8857 Commercial Avenue. The establishment was advertised as having a "nationally famous collection of curios." Prohibition changed the lives of many of these local figures.

Kompare's Tavern was located at 8908 Green Bay in the "Millgate" section of South Chicago. It catered to particular ethnic groups (Slovenians and Croatians) and provided rooms and meeting facilities. Many taverns in the mill communities were rooming houses. Often an immigrant father would come to the United States alone to work and save money to send for his family at a later date.

Walton's Saloon at 92nd and South Chicago Avenue was the scene of many South Chicago political and business deals. Some taverns were "stand-up" taverns. Note the lack of furniture and the presence of the spittoons on the floor of this stand-up tavern.

Hickey's Lounge was located at 9185 South Chicago Avenue. Pictured are representatives of the Budweiser Company with local tavern owners. The man in the short-sleeved shirt is Leo Rolek, owner of the tavern across the street at 2911 East 92nd Street.

The Evangelical Lutheran Church, now known as Immanuel Lutheran, is located on 90th and Houston Avenue. It is one of the oldest churches in South Chicago and was founded by German Lutherans in 1873. This post card view shows the original church and the new church built in 1907. Notice the horse and wagon in the lower left portion of the picture.

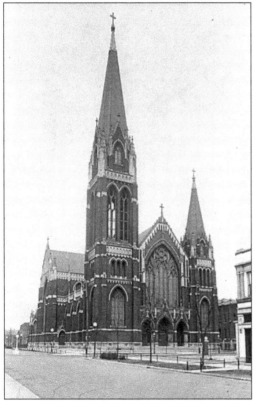

Saint Michael the Archangel was a Polish-Catholic parish and was founded in 1892, to serve the growing Polish population of the area. It is located at the corner of 83rd and South Shore Drive and is one of the most impressive structures on the Southeast Side. Father Paul Rhode was pastor when this building was constructed in 1907. He became the first bishop of Polish origin in the United States in 1908, and remained at Saint Michael's until 1915.

49

Our Lady of Guadalupe is the oldest Mexican parish in Chicago and was founded in 1923. This photo shows the first building used as a church by the parish. It served the needs of the parish until 1928, when a new church was dedicated. The first church building was located at 9024 Mackinaw Avenue.

Ground was broken for a school for Our Lady of Guadalupe Parish, and a cornerstone was laid on October 12, 1947. The school enrollment continues to grow, and the school continues to thrive in an era when many parochial schools are closing. Mexicans are the fastest growing ethnic group on the Southeast side at present.

Bowen School was built in 1876, at the corner of 93rd and Houston. There were five teachers on the faculty at that time. As the population of the area grew, a new school became necessary and was built at 2710 East 89th Street. It opened in 1910. Pictured is an English class from Bowen High School in 1936.

There were several Catholic High Schools in Southeast Chicago. Most have closed. Pictured is a group from the 1940 class of St. Michael's School. St. Michael's was a high school for girls that closed in the late 1960s.

Numerous special events were held in South Chicago. One of the most popular was when the circus came to town. This is a photo of a 1912 circus parade that marched down 92nd Street. This particular event was sponsored by the Goodfellows Club of United States Steel South Works.

The oldest Mexican Independence Day Parade in the city of Chicago has been held in South Chicago since the late 1930s. This annual event continues to be held and is a social highlight of the year for the community. This photo shows Queen Stella Diaz on a float in the 1939 parade.

Social organizations were common in the Southeast Side communities. Many were organized along ethnic or religious lines. The Young Ladies' Sodality of Our Lady of Guadalupe Parish, pictured here in 1944, was one such group.

Ethnic culture was preserved and passed down through the efforts of many groups. This is reflected in this picture of Croatian dancers in ethnic costumes at Marquette Gardens, a local banquet and meeting hall located at 83rd and Marquette Avenue.

The Boys Alliance Club Drum and Bugle Corps was organized in 1933, and its musical director was Stanley M. Pinski. The Corps membership rose to 70 musicians by 1936, and the group won numerous awards. It won the State Fair title in 1937, and for several years won the Chicago Tribune Chicagoland Music Festival, Juvenile Division. The picture shows the band in 1934.

The unions were among the most important organizations in the community. They were important not only for workplace issues but also for political reasons and social activities. They were organizations that crossed over ethnic and religious lines. Pictured is a social event sponsored by Local 65, United Steel Workers of America.

Strong family structure was a hallmark of the Southeast Side neighborhoods. Large families were also very common. This is the Castro family of Our Lady of Guadalupe Parish in the late 1940s.

Eight of the twelve children of Joseph and Agnes Olejnik are pictured here. The Olejnik family, of Polish ethnicity, was typical of many South Chicago families. Joseph worked at United States Steel for over fifty years, and the family lived at several different South Chicago addresses, all of which were within walking distance of the steel mill.

The steel mills provided good wages and an opportunity for immigrants to achieve the American dream. Part of that dream was to own a house or, better yet, a two-flat or three-flat. Pictured is the interior of a typical steelworker's home in the early 1900s. Notice the telephone and gas fixtures.

The prosperity of the 1920s is reflected in this picture of the Olejnik family on a Sunday outing. Ownership of a car was another indicator of success. The steel mills provided a good living to those who were willing to work hard. Another factor in the ability of an average worker to own a car was the affordability of the Model T.

Many activities took place in the backyards of family houses. In the days before backyard swimming pools, a washtub served as a way to cool off on a hot summer day. Pictured is the author in the backyard of his grandparents home at 8718 Baltimore in South Chicago in 1947.

South Chicago had a small African-American community near the south entrance to South Works as early as the turn of the century. During the Great Migrations, large numbers of African Americans moved into the communities of the Southeast Side. In recent years, African Americans have become the majority population in the communities of South Chicago and South Deering.

South Chicago celebrated the Bicentennial of the United States in 1976 with numerous events. Above is a photo taken during the Bicentennial Parade down Commercial Avenue. At a town meeting during the 1976 Bicentennial activities, the idea of creating the Southeast Historical Society (originally the East Side Historical Society) was first discussed.

There was an attempt to portray the Calumet River as more than a working river. As part of the Bicentennial celebration, a regatta was held on the Calumet River, showing its potential for recreational activities. Pictured are two competitors in the Central States Amateur Rowing Association's 69th Annual Championship Regatta held on June 27, 1976.

BESSEMER PARK—SOUTH CHICAGO, ILL. 239-8.

Each of the Southeast Side communities has a major park within its boundaries. The largest park in South Chicago was Bessemer Park, named after the developer of an early steel-making process. This post card view shows an early bicycle-racing track in Bessemer Park.

Bicycling was also a leisure activity for community residents, as seen in this 1896 photo from the South Chicago YMCA. Note the clothing worn by the cyclists; it is a far cry from the athletic wear of today.

The Sundodgers were a legendary local baseball team. Many neighborhood sports heroes played for the Sundodgers. The team was organized in the 1930s in South Chicago and played most of their games at Bessemer Park. They later moved to the East Side where they were sponsored by the Illiana American Legion Post.

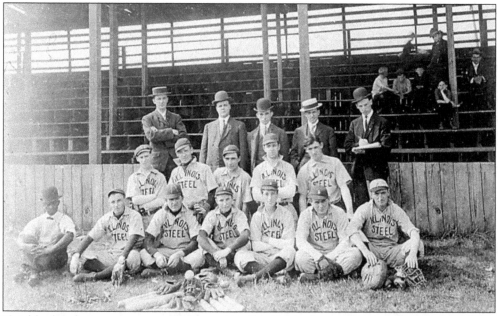

Neighborhood sports teams provided recreational activities for community residents. Many area companies and businesses promoted these teams. United States Steel sponsored many teams in many different sports. Pictured is a 1906 baseball team from Illinois Steel South Works. There was a baseball field on South Works property at one time.

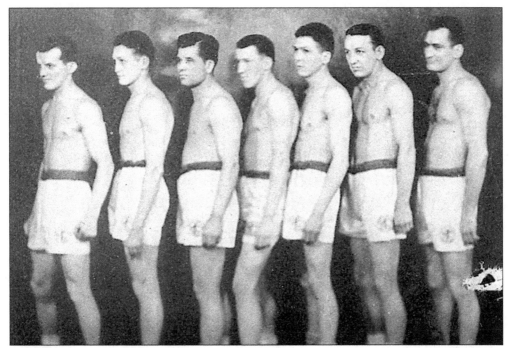

South Works sponsored a boxing team that had a big rivalry with other U.S. Steel plants, especially the plant in Gary, Indiana. One of the best-known of the U.S. Steel boxers was Gene Spencer. Spencer was a professional boxer from 1937 to 1951. He had a record of 90 wins, 28 losses, and 50 draws. He continued to work at the mill while boxing and retired after 40 years. Gene Spencer is fifth from the left in this 1937 photo of the South Works boxing team.

Four neighborhood boxing legends get together at Calumet Park at a local boxing event c. 1980. From left to right are Gene Spencer, Philomena Zale, Henry Lenard, Ted Ross, and Tony Zale. Henry Lenard was Gene Spencer's boxing coach at the South Chicago YMCA in 1931.

Often, sports teams were organized along ethnic lines. The Yaquis were a baseball team comprised primarily of Mexican ball players. They were well respected for their abilities and had a reputation as one of the area's top baseball teams. Pictured are the 1937 Yaquis.

Churches and religious organizations also sponsored sports teams and leagues. This is a softball team sponsored by the Santa Maria Knights of Columbus. They were the 1937 South Chicago Commercial League champions.

Four

SOUTH DEERING

South Deering dates its origins from 1845, but the history of the community is tied to the mill built along the Calumet River near 109th Street in 1875. Both the mill and the community were initially known as Brown's Mill. Later the community came to be called Irondale, although this was never the official name of the community. In 1882, the name of the post office was changed to Cummings. Key events in the early years of the community were the construction of Chittenden Road east of the Calumet River and the coming of several railroad lines to the area. After Brown's Mill was built, South Deering grew steadily. Other industries came to the area and built near the river or along Torrence Avenue. Among them were General Mills, Chicago Steel and Wire Company, and By Products Coke Corporation.

The South Deering residential area measures only one-half-square mile of the community's 6-square mile total area. In 1938, new federal measures supported improvements in the community, like the paving and widening of 103rd Street to encourage new residential construction. The upgrading of the residential area north of 103rd became the Calumet Gardens housing development and was later called Jeffery Manor. In 1938, the Public Works Administration built Trumbull Park Homes and leased it to the Chicago Housing Authority. In recent years, the community has seen hard times, especially with the closing of Wisconsin Steel. Some of the richest wetland areas in Chicago are located in South Deering.

Pictured is the South Deering Improvement Association float from the 1938 Fourth of July parade.

Torrence Avenue, shown here at 106th Street looking north, was named after General J.T. Torrence, an early stockholder in the Joseph H. Brown Mill. The intersection of 106th and Torrence was the crossroads of South Deering. The first building housed the South Deering Pleasure and Athletic Club, the next was Schoenfield's Hardware, and the next was Vi and Coy's Tavern.

The main shopping district in South Deering was concentrated around the intersection of 106th Street and Torrence Avenue. Businesses and residences were located on the west side of the street and ran south. On the east side of the street was the huge Wisconsin Steel Plant. The South Deering trolley can be seen in the view.

The section of the community closest to the mill was known as Irondale, although this was never the official name of the community. Workers at the mill often lived in this section because they could walk to work. This is in sharp contrast to the present when so many people live far from work and spend great amounts of time commuting. Pictured are houses on 105th and Calhoun in Irondale.

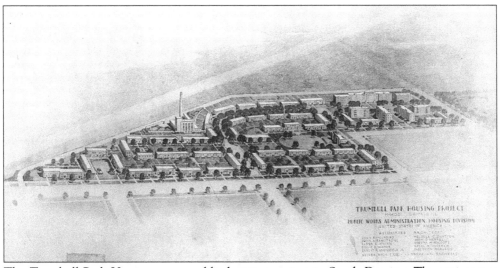

The Trumbull Park Homes were a public housing project in South Deering. The project was built in 1937, south of Trumbull Park. The homes were a project constructed by the Public Works Administration (PWA), Housing Division. They were an example of low-rise public housing, which proved to be much more successful than the high-rise public housing projects built in Chicago during the 1950s and 1960s.

The most important social event in South Deering was the Fourth of July Celebration at Trumbull Park, sponsored by the South Deering Improvement Association. This photo of the 1938 parade shows a marching band on Torrence Avenue across the street from Wisconsin Steel.

Daily Calumet

rld's Greatest   Inland Seaport

GO, ILL., TUESDAY, JULY 3, 1962

Price 5c Home Delivery 30c per week

WEATHER

Partly cloudy and warmer today with scattered thundershowers likely, high in 80s. Tonight chance of showers, low near 70. Wednesday partly sunny, warm, humid, chance of thundershowers, high in upper 80s.

Expect 40,000 At July 4 Fete In So. Deering

This headline from the *The Daily Calumet*, a community newspaper, shows the popularity of the Fourth of July activities in South Deering. The day's activities included a parade, beauty contest, sports activities, and a huge fireworks display at Trumbull Park.

The Calumet Bakery, located at 2510 East 106th Street, was founded by Matt Pocernich, a Croatian immigrant. Matt had worked for another Chicago bakery during the Depression, but in 1938 he took "the one thing he knew how to do" and opened his own business. The bakery is still open and operated by the family.

In all the area neighborhoods, taverns clustered near the entrances to the mills. It was not unusual to find workers after a night shift having a shot and a beer at 7 a.m. This is John's tavern located at 109th and Torrence Avenue across the street from Wisconsin Steel.

Hrv. Kat. Crkva Presv. Srca. Isusova u. So. Chicago Ill.
R. Cath. Croation Church. Sacr. Heart of Jesus So. Chicago Ill.
-1914-

Croatians who came to the Southeast Side worshipped at Saint George's Church, a Slovenian-Catholic church on the East Side. When their numbers grew they established a Croatian-Catholic church in the South Deering community. Pictured is the original Sacred Heart Church, built in 1914, which was replaced by a new church in 1964.

Saint Archangel Michael Serbian Orthodox Church was founded in 1919. This picture shows the first building owned by the parish, which had been bought from a Danish-Lutheran group. The parish recently sold its property in South Deering and moved to Lansing, Illinois.

Students in South Deering were originally served by the Marsh Branch elementary school at 10710 South Calhoun. Groundbreaking for a new school was held in 1922. Orville T. Bright School, at 10740 South Calhoun, was completed and dedicated on January 1, 1924. This is a photo of the school's second graduating class in June 1925.

Elementary school class pictures are a great way to bring back memories. This is a photo of the seventh and eighth grade students of Saint Kevin's School in 1938. In spite of adverse economic conditions, the class had an optimistic outlook about the future.

Family events and celebrations were important in all of the Southeast Side neighborhoods. Pictured are Lucille Savastano and Norene DeCristofano dressed for a family wedding in 1942.

Families from Irondale rented a bus for an excursion to Wisconsin in 1947. Weekend trips to nearby states were a common form of relaxation.

Churches did more than meet the religious needs of their members. They also were important providers of social activities and contacts. Pictured is a church picnic from St. Kevin's Church, held at Egger's Grove on the East Side in June 1947.

One of South Deering's most popular ethnic clubs was the Roman Knights, organized in 1932. Original members of the club were all Italian Americans. Pictured at the Annual Reunion Dinner on November 3, 1979, from left to right, are Dr. Romeo Pallotto, Joseph DeLaurentis, Sam Carnavacciola, Daniel Guadagno, John Battistella Jr., Michael Pallotto Jr., James Guadagno, and Alex Savastano.

The Karageorgevich Lodge was an organization for young Serbian men founded in 1905. The lodge members gave money and moral support to the people of their homeland. The photo shows members of the group in 1912.

In the Southeast Side neighborhoods, almost any type of ethnic music could be found. The Saint Michael Archangel Tamburitzans, pictured above in 1967, was composed of performers from 10 to 17 years of age. They were organized in 1963 by Slavo Lazich and directed by Martin Kapugi. They performed at many local events.

Five

EAST SIDE

The East Side began in 1851 and derives its name from the fact that it is located on the east side of the Calumet River. One of the early names used for the area was the "Island" because of its location between Lake Michigan, the Calumet River, and Wolf Lake on the south. A plaque on the 92nd Street Bridge commemorates a pontoon toll bridge located at that point across the Calumet River, connecting the East Side to what later became the South Chicago community. Much of the early history of the East Side is affected by the development of South Chicago, an older and larger community to the north. The first railroad station in the area at 100th Street and Ewing Avenue was not built until 1873. Like the other communities on the Southeast Side, it did not develop in earnest until industrialization began after the Civil War. The real boom period for the East Side occurred after World War II when housing was built on the south end of the community to help meet the demands of the "Baby Boomers."

The photo shows the East Side Businessman's Association, family, and friends in 1924.

An early East Side pioneer, Andreas von Zirngibl, was a fisherman who came to the East Side in the early 1850s. He died in 1855, and his heirs buried him on the banks of the Calumet River near 92nd Street in what had once been a Native-American burial ground. A long series of court battles with developers resulted in a decision that guaranteed access to the grave in perpetuity. This photo shows the condition of the grave *c.* 1940.

The East Side Historical Society (now the Southeast Historical Society) renovated the Von Zirngibl gravesite. Society members Richard and Robert Sell, Henry Zirngibl, great grandson of Andreas, and others were among the workers on the project. The grave was rededicated on July 26, 1987. Pictured are workers resetting the headstone.

Another important landmark on the East Side is the State Line Boundary Marker. It marks the boundary between Illinois and Indiana and was erected in the 1830s, probably making it the oldest landmark in Chicago. It is currently in the process of being designated an official City of Chicago Landmark. This photo shows a father and his two sons viewing the marker c. 1915.

In 1988 Tom Rutkowski, a member of the East Side Historical Society, initiated a project which resulted in the restoration of the State Line Boundary Marker. It also was moved 192 feet due north of its original location at the entrance of the State Line Generating Station. A small park, named Alan Benson Park, was constructed. Benson was a neighborhood resident who worked at the power station and worked to have the marker restored. The above photo shows the moving of the marker by crews from Commonwealth Edison.

This early 1900s view of Ewing Avenue looks south from 99th Street. As with South Chicago, the early development in the neighborhood started along the Calumet River and then moved away from the river. The original shopping district on the East Side and much of the earliest housing was located in the north end of the community once referred to as "Taylorville."

As the East Side grew, development moved south across the railroad tracks that paralleled Indianapolis Boulevard. As settlement moved into this area, commercial development followed. This photo shows Ewing Avenue south of 100th Street, the location of the train station, in the early 1900s.

Initially, as seen in the photo, the area around 106th and Ewing Avenue was primarily residential. Later, this became the main shopping district for the East Side. Mausen's Tavern, originally the Baker and Bauman Saloon, was located at the northeast corner of 106th and Ewing Avenue. When this photo was taken, Willy's Hardware on the left across the street and the tavern on the right were the only businesses on what was chiefly a residential street.

In later years, the intersection of 106th and Ewing, shown here, became the heart of the East Side shopping district. The original home of the East Side Bank was down the block in a building that formerly housed the East Side Theater. In the 1960s, Mausen's Tavern was demolished to enlarge the bank parking lot.

The growth of the shopping district is evident in this photo taken in the mid-1960s during Old Fashioned Days. Visible in the scene are East Side Recreation, a four-lane bowling alley, the Ben Franklin Store, a "dime store," and Cohen's, a clothing store.

One of the East Side's most anticipated summer social events was Old Fashioned Days, sponsored by the East Side Chamber of Commerce. Pictured is a typical Old Fashioned Days Celebration held in the mid-1960s. Music, food, and shopping bargains were readily available during the event.

Dr. Walter Titzel was a local general practitioner who delivered thousands of babies. His office, shown here in 1890, was located at 10150 Ewing Avenue. Dr. Titzel delivered babies until he was 77 years of age, and he maintained a journal to record his deliveries. He listed 4,169 births in the journal from 1888 to November 1942.

Neighborhood grocery stores often catered to particular ethnic groups. Large numbers of Italians lived on the north end of the East Side. Milano's Grocery Store at 9550 Avenue N served this group. Pictured, from left to right, are Albert Milano, son of Santa Milano, John Zappa, son-in-law of Santa Milano, and Santa Milano.

Neighborhood ice cream parlors and "soda shops" were favorite destinations for anyone with a sweet tooth. This is a view of the interior of Ernie's Ice Cream Parlor at 10052 Ewing Avenue c. 1924.

The numerous taverns and saloons in the area received their deliveries by horse-drawn wagons in the days before the automotive age. Often, they were supplied with beer brewed in local breweries. Pictured is a delivery from United Brewery at 100th Street and Avenue N. Prohibition would put a stop to this type of scene on neighborhood streets.

Avenue H., looking North from 99th Street, South Chicago, Ill.

This early 1900s postcard view is labeled as 99th and Avenue H but is currently 99th and Avenue J. The church in the background is the First Church Evangelical Association, the second church organized on the East Side in 1875.

Kreiter Avenue is a little known street on the East Side. It runs parallel to Ewing Avenue from 93rd to 95th Street and is one of the shortest streets in Chicago. This is a picture of a residence at 9307 Kreiter in 1909. At one time the house is said to have served as a lighthouse marking the entrance to the Calumet River.

The East Side was part of the Village of Hyde Park until 1889, when it joined the City of Chicago. One of the benefits of joining the city was receiving city services like police and fire services. Pictured are early East Side firemen with Captain Charles Stengel.

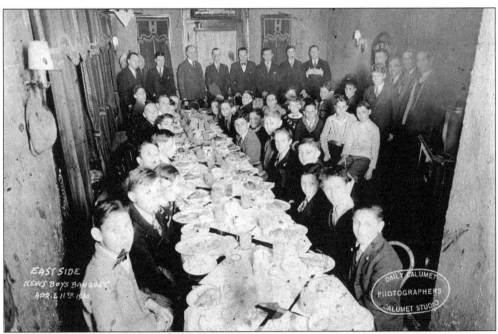

A familiar neighborhood sight was the newspaper boy delivering newspapers by foot or on bicycle. Deliveries came twice a day, in the morning for the *Tribune* and *Sun Times* and in the afternoon for the *Daily News* and the *Herald American*. And, of course, they also delivered *The Daily Calumet*. Pictured are East Side newspaper boys at a banquet on April 11, 1930.

Local politicians and community leaders seldom missed the groundbreaking ceremonies for local improvements. Pictured is a groundbreaking that took place on October 28, 1930, for a neighborhood playground located at 108th and Avenue H.

By April 23, 1938, the date of this groundbreaking for new homes at 109th and Avenue J, residential development on the East Side had spread to the south portion of the community. Many marshy areas had to be filled in before construction could proceed. Some constructions, mostly apartment buildings, took place in the late 1920s. Due to the Depression, it was not until the 1940s that large numbers of single family homes were constructed.

The second-oldest church on the East Side, the United Methodist Church, has had three locations over its existence. First located on 99th and Avenue J, the congregation built a new church at 10323 Ewing in 1915, and then moved to 110th and Ewing in 1955. The photo shows the members of the church's Chancel Choir.

In June of 1876, the East Side Baptist Church was opened at 107th Street and Avenue N. Pictured is a group of women at the church in 1920. At the rear of the church, a privy can be seen. The church is one of the oldest on the East Side.

Saint George's Catholic Church was founded by Slovenians in 1903. Originally the parish also served the area's Italian community and Croatian Catholics until they built their own parish, Sacred Heart, in nearby South Deering. Pictured is the 1919 Confirmation Class of Saint George's Parish.

Annunciata Catholic Church was founded in 1941. It is a territorial parish, which means that it has defined geographical boundaries and has always served a multicultural population. The first religious service held for the parish took place in a garage owned by a local builder. The "Wooden Church" pictured above was built at a cost of $11,000 and was dedicated on June 21, 1942. A new church was built in 1970.

Neighborhood schools were important social institutions in the community. This is a photo of the entire student body of Saint Francis De Sales elementary school in 1895. The priest is Father Diekman, and the nun is Sister Appolonia.

Douglas Taylor Elementary School is named after an early real estate developer on the East Side. The original school building, pictured here, was located on 99th and Avenue J. A new school building opened in 1924 on 99th and Avenue H.

This is a picture of room number four from Gallistel School, the oldest public elementary school on the East Side. The photo was taken shortly before the class went to Jackson Park to see the World's Columbian Exposition (World's Fair) in 1893. The class's teacher is Miss Taylor.

Annunciata Elementary School opened in September of 1949, with eight classrooms. By the early 1950s there were 560 students in enrollment. In an era when many private schools are closing due to declining enrollments, Annunciata is open and thriving. This is a photo of the 1960 eighth grade boys' class. At this time the boys' and girls' classes were separated in the upper grades.

Pictured is the George Washington High School marching band performing at half time during a football game at Eckersall Stadium. The Minutemen marching band won numerous prestigious awards under the direction of Salvatore Grasso.

The major annual social event for the East Side was the Labor Day Celebration. Events included a parade, beauty contest, and other activities, which were held at Calumet Park. Drum and bugle corps from throughout the Midwest participated. Pictured is a float sponsored by the East Side Chamber of Commerce in the 1985 parade during the organization's 60th Anniversary.

Calumet Park was the site of many community recreational activities. Here, the U.S. Steel South Works Orchestra practices for a recital at Calumet Park. Virtually every department of the mill was represented by members of the orchestra.

A small toboggan slide was built at Calumet Park in its early years. Calumet Park was built on landfill, made up mostly of slag. The park and most of the surrounding area is flat, so this structure gave residents an opportunity to enjoy sledding.

Lake Michigan was not only a transportation magnet for heavy industry but also provided recreational opportunities for area residents. Pictured is a beach scene at Calumet Park in the early 1900s.

Many neighborhood teens worked as lifeguards at area pools and beaches. Pictured is the lifeguard crew at Calumet Park Beach in 1945. According to the donor of the picture, most of the boys pictured here were in the service the following year. He also said, "Swimming in the lake in April and May and rowing a life boat was exciting with high waves."

Neighborhood sports teams drew numerous fans to area parks and created local legends. Pictured is the 1929 East Side Robins baseball team based at Calumet Park from 1927 to 1935. This particular team won its first 17 games and finished the season with a 22 and 3 record.

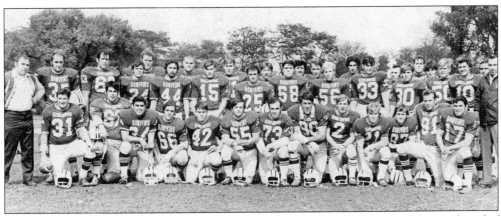

The Bonivirs were a social and athletic club originally organized for Italians on the north end of the East Side. They were organized in 1917, and were formally chartered in 1924. This is a team photo of the 1970 Bonivirs football team. Southeast Side residents are sure to remember other local football teams like Chuck Motors, the Trumbull Park Blues, and Marty and Joe's Chiefs.

Scouting organizations provided supervised activities to the children of the community. Pictured are District 19 Girl Scout volunteers from the East Side and Hegewisch who were honored at a Volunteer Recognition Luncheon. They are, from left to right: (seated) Pat Lewantowski, Mary Ellen DeMercede, Lucille Wojtas, Julie Curran, and Henrietta Oberman; (standing) LaVerne Jar, Ora Coon, Marie Jervis, and Evelyn Clarke.

Sokol clubs were organized along ethnic lines. They were social and athletic organizations. Sokol Club was organized August 30, 1903, by Bohemian immigrants. The group built their hall at 108th and Green Bay in 1909. They were active in gymnastics and drills and conducted all their business in the Bohemian language until 1940.

Six

HEGEWISCH

Hegewisch is the youngest of the four Southeast Side communities. A. Hegewisch, the head of U.S. Rolling Stock Company, founded it in 1883. There is some confusion about Mr. Hegewisch's first name. Some early sources refer to him as Achilles, and others use the name Adolph. Hegewisch wanted to develop a town loosely patterned on the nearby town of Pullman. The plan was to build a factory to construct railroad cars and to sell land for houses in the vicinity of the plant. Brainard Avenue and the railroad tracks that paralleled the street divided the factory property from the housing area. Unlike the Pullman situation where the company retained ownership of the housing, U.S. Rolling Stock sold lots to homeowners. The town was not initially as successful as Pullman was and large-scale population growth did not occur until later.

Hegewisch was also geographically isolated from the other three Southeast Side communities by Hyde Lake and wetland areas. It was easier for Hegewisch residents to go to northwest Indiana, especially the town of Hammond, than it was for them to go to the East Side or to South Chicago. When Hegewisch residents said they were going "downtown" they meant to downtown Hammond; their Goldblatt's store was also in Hammond.

The first link between Hegewisch and the rest of Chicago was the trolley that ran over the wetlands of Hyde Lake to the East Side. Prior to this transportation link, the community had stronger ties to Hammond, Indiana, than to Chicago. The trolley operated a limited schedule, and if a commuter missed the last trolley of the day, he was fated to spend the night in a different neighborhood.

In 1936, a Hegewisch resident named John Serafin built this radio tower called the Beacon, supposedly to set up a local radio station. Serafin was injured during construction, and the tower never went into operation. It was eventually sold to the funeral parlor next door for a parking lot. Some area businesses are still named for the Beacon.

The Hegewisch Opera House was a theater where musical and dramatic presentations drew patrons from surrounding communities. This is a rare view of the interior of the Opera House hosting an event for the Pressed Steel Company of Hegewisch.

Railroads were probably more important to the development of Hegewisch than to the other southeast communities. The community was founded because of railroads, and railroad tracks defined the residential sections of the community. This is one of many railroad intersections in Hegewisch.

The South Shore and South Bend Railroad stopped in Hegewisch on its way to downtown Chicago from northwest Indiana. This is the old South Shore station on Brandon Avenue. Even today the South Shore carries commuters from Hegewisch and Indiana to Chicago.

Wolf Lake is a recreational area that straddles the Illinois and Indiana border. The official dedication of the state park on the Illinois side of the lake took place at the beginning of Indian Creek on October 13, 1946. A stone obelisk commemorates the dedication by Illinois Governor Dwight Green, shown above.

In 1833, a young Army Corps of Engineers officer, Lieutenant Jefferson Davis, recommended improvements in the Calumet River. Among the improvements was connection to the Mississippi River system. This was done in 1922, when the Cal Sag Channel was completed with controlling locks near Blue Island. In 1956, the Cal Sag Channel was widened and the larger O'Brien Locks were built at about 134th Street on the Calumet River. Pictured is the dedication of the O'Brien Locks in 1959.

In July 1983, Hegewisch celebrated its Centennial with a series of events. One of the events was the Hegewisch Centennial Parade. Shown here is the float, sponsored by the Hegewisch Chamber of Commerce, carrying contestants for the Miss Hegewisch contest.

Neighborhood residents enjoyed sitting and socializing on front porches or in front of area businesses. Pictured is a group of men and boys engaged in this activity in Hegewisch in the 1920s.

The main shopping strip in Hegewisch ran along Baltimore Avenue (first named South Chicago Avenue, later Erie Avenue) from 132nd street to 135th Street. Additional stores were located on Brandon Avenue. Pictured are early businesses in this commercial district.

Pictured are the Morelli Ice Cream Store and a Barber Shop and Bath establishment. This was a very important business, especially in the days before most homes had indoor plumbing. Note the wooden sidewalks and dirt streets of Baltimore Avenue.

The Sowa grocery store was located at 13129 Baltimore. Behind the counter is butcher Albert Sowa Jr. The Sowa family was involved in several family-run businesses in Hegewisch.

There were a number of small grocery stores in all of the Southeast Side neighborhoods. This is an exterior view of Emma's Food Shoppe at 13309 Baltimore Avenue in 1952.

Moll's originally opened as a saloon but eventually developed into a restaurant. It was a family business started by Joseph Moll in 1911, and later taken over by George Moll. This exterior view was taken in the early 1920s. Moll's was located at 13358 Houston Avenue.

This interior view of the South Shore Inn, a popular local tavern located at 13611 Brainard, was taken in the early 1940s. Pictured from left to right are: Joe Frank, owner Marian Gersevich and wife, Mike Sowa, Mary Ubik, John Sowa, unidentified, Mrs. Frank, Joe Yurko, three unidentified people, and Mary Lakeman.

Swedish Lutherans living in Hegewisch founded the Swedish Evangelical Lebanon Lutheran Church on January 17, 1896. The first church, shown here with members of the congregation, was located at 132nd and Brandon Avenue. A new church was built in 1970 and in 1996, Lebanon Lutheran Church celebrated its 100th Anniversary.

In February 1924, a meeting occurred which led to the founding of Assumption Greek Orthodox Church in Hegewisch. The first church building burned down in a fire in 1936. A new church was built the following year and expanded in 1967. The Greek community in Hegewisch continues to thrive. Pictured are members of the church at a Christmas Dinner in 1935.

Saint Hedwig's is a Polish National Catholic church founded in 1940. The Polish National Catholic Church developed in the 1890s out of a conflict within the Roman Catholic Church in the United States. It was formed in Buffalo, New York in 1897, and has had a Chicago presence since its founding. This is a picture of Saint Hedwig's Church in Hegewisch.

Saint Columba Catholic Church was a territorial parish that served Hegewisch. It was founded in 1884, and was the first Catholic church in the community. Pictured is the First Communion Confirmation Class from the Silver Jubilee year of 1909. The parish was founded by Father Timothy O' Sullivan.

Henry Clay was the public elementary school serving the Hegewisch community. Pictured is a group of students in front of the school in 1942.

This is a picture of the first graduating class from Saint Florian Elementary School in 1912. The priest in the photo, Father Florian Chodniewicz, organized the parish for Polish Catholics in 1905. The school opened in 1908, and by 1920 had an enrollment of 500 students. Father Chodniewicz was killed in the rectory by an intruder on January 27, 1922.

The main park facility in Hegewisch is Mann Park. Pictured is the dedication ceremony for Mann Park in 1931. Mayor Richard J. Daley's last official act as mayor was the dedication of a new gymnasium and field house at Mann Park on December 20, 1976. He suffered a heart attack later that day and died.

During the Cold War, there was a Nike Missile Base in Hegewisch at Wolf Lake. This monument commemorates the base and Veteran's Memorial Markers at Wolf Lake. The monument was dedicated on September 18, 1999.

Seven

PROBLEMS AND PROTESTS

Although the Southeast Side typifies an American success story, there were numerous problems faced by local residents. Some were unique to the area, others were faced by most Americans. Fire was a constant threat to homes, churches, business, and industry. The Depression of the 1930s left its mark on this community as it did throughout the rest of nation. Workers lost their jobs or faced severely curtailed hours, and many lost their homes. Area businesses and banks went out of business. Industrial unions were organized in the face of stiff opposition. But the community survived the economic hard times only to face another challenge, World War II. The Southeast Side, as it had in the First World War, contributed to the war effort in many ways. Area residents served in the Armed Forces, and many did not return. Those who did not serve in the military became part of the "Home Front." More recently, there were problems with racial change in the communities, and a grass-roots environmental movement fought the spread of landfills and industrial pollution. The decline of the steel industry in the '70s and '80s severely curtailed the region's economy. And the Southeast Side fought the City of Chicago's plan to build a Lake Calumet Airport in the area.

In the photo above, striking CIO union workers stand outside a shed during one of the many strikes that have occurred in mills and factories on Chicago's Southeast Side.

Fire was a constant threat to the wooden two-flats and three-flats in local neighborhoods. This picture of a fire, which occurred in the Bush on July 23, 1919, shows the extensive damage suffered by area residences. Saint Michael's Catholic Church looms in the background.

Business structures were also struck by fire with devastating consequences. This fire occurred at 3024 East 92nd Street on a winter Sunday morning in 1916. The Greenwald Furniture Store and the Pacini Candy & Cigar Store were destroyed.

Grain elevators, most of which were located along the Calumet River, were particularly vulnerable to fire. This fire occurred on August 3, 1908. Notice the swing bridge in the foreground.

Grain elevator fires are often set off when a spark ignites the grain dust in the elevator. This spectacular fire burned an elevator between 102nd and 103rd Street on the west side of the Calumet River on May 11, 1939. The picture shows the huge crowd that gathered to watch the spectacular fire.

Fires were very common in area churches. This is a picture of the remains of Bethlehem Lutheran Church at 103rd and Avenue H after a fire. The church burned on Maundy (Holy) Thursday in 1918.

This view of the interior of Saint Francis De Sales church shows the extensive damage caused by a fire on January 22, 1925. It is said that the fire destroyed not only the church but also the health of the parish's pastor, Father John P. Suerth. Other area churches also suffered losses due to fire. Immaculate Conception in South Chicago burned in 1883 and again in 1894. In May of 1902, Saint Patrick's Church was destroyed by fire.

One of the goals of many Southeast Siders was to own their own homes, or better yet, a two-flat or three-flat. The famous Chicago Bungalow was a housing style that made this a reality for many working-class families. This is a bungalow at 8506 Baltimore owned by Joseph Olejnik and family. The family lost their home during the Depression, as did many other families.

Calumet National Bank was part of a group of area banks that closed during the Great Depression. Other Southeast Side banks in the group were East Side Trust and Savings Bank, Hegewisch State Bank, and Interstate National Bank.

One of the most important events in American labor history is the "Memorial Day Massacre" that occurred at Republic Steel on Memorial Day, May 30, 1937. This sculpture stands at the approximate location of this event. It is mistakenly called the "Memorial Day Massacre Sculpture;" however, the company erected it with the following interpretation in mind: the six long bars symbolize Republic's six steel districts, the four bars mark the cardinal compass points, and the spiral bar signifies the bond between Republic and its neighbors.

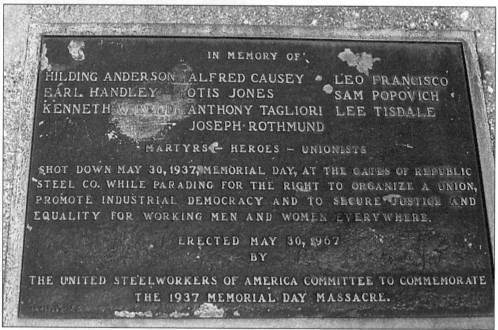

The only commemoration of the "Memorial Day Massacre" is a plaque at the foot of a flag pole in the parking lot of United Steel Workers Local 1033. The plaque lists the names of the ten men who lost their lives in the massacre.

When the United States entered World War I and World War II, Southeast Siders joined other Americans in the war effort. This picture shows a local resident plowing a war garden with a tractor loaned by the International Harvester Company during World War I.

This photo shows children collecting cans during World War I. The picture was taken in October 1917, at 106th and Hoxie. Pictured are Vic Rea, Bruno Uchman, Tom Flynn, Fran Datch, Pat Orlando, and the little girl is Mary Orlando.

When war occurred, the area mills went into high production. Rallies and campaigns were held to encourage workers to increase production levels and to purchase war bonds or liberty bonds. This is a photo of a Liberty Bond Rally at Pressed Steel in Hegewisch in 1918.

When World War I ended on Armistice Day, November 11, 1918, workers at Western Steel and Foundry in Hegewisch celebrated outside the factory.

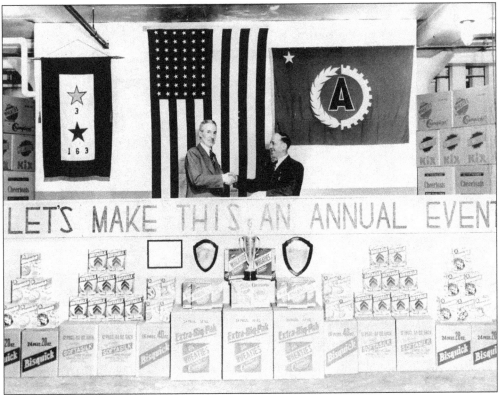

Area plants received awards from the government for high production during the war. Pictured is a General Mills official receiving an "A" award pennant on March 28, 1945. On the left is a flag showing that 163 employees were serving in the military and three employees had been killed in action. During the war, General Mills produced dry soup for the military. The employees called it "Russian Soup" because of its intended destination.

Pressed Steel in Hegewisch produced railroad cars before the war. During World War II, they converted to the production of tanks. Here, a tank rolls off the production line at Pressed Steel.

Parades, bond drives, and other rallies served to keep up morale during the war. This is a photo of a 1942 Civil Defense parade on the 8700 block of Commercial Avenue.

During World War II, many women joined the work force in jobs that were previously closed to them. Thousands were recruited for area steel mills. Referred to as "Rosie the Riveter," each woman contributed much to the war effort. Pictured are several "Rosies" working on a track gang at U.S. Steel during the war.

Many blocks had displays to honor the residents of the block serving in the Armed Forces. This is a South Chicago display from 1944.

This victory display was located at 131st and Baltimore Avenue in Hegewisch. The photo was taken in 1943.

Even children contributed to the war effort. Paper drives and scrap metal drives gave kids an opportunity to help out. Pictured are Maxine and Patricia Olejnik with paper they collected for a paper drive.

Kids could also give their moral support to the war effort. From left to right, Richard, Maxine, Patricia, and Geraldine Olejnik show their support for the cause.

Personal plans were put on hold or altered because of the war. This is the 1944 wedding of Florence and Edward "Buck" Sellers. The South Chicago couple was married at Camp White in Oregon shortly before the groom was shipped out to the Philippines and Okinawa. After the war, the couple moved to the East Side and contributed to the "Baby Boom" with ten children.

The war brought ration stamps and long lines to the home front. Pictured is a line outside an A&P store at 133rd and Baltimore in Hegewisch. The crowd was waiting to buy soap and coffee.

During the Vietnam Conflict, 12 young men from Our Lady of Guadalupe Parish in South Chicago were killed in action. According to area veterans, no other parish in the country suffered more combat deaths. This is a picture of a mural across the street from the church, commemorating the sacrifices of these heroes.

Racial change did not come easily to the Southeast Side. When the first African-American family moved into the Trumbull Park Homes in South Deering in 1953, violence broke out in the community. This headline from *The Daily Calumet* of August 29, 1953, reflects the problems that occurred.

Wisconsin Steel closed on March 28, 1980, after over one hundred years of steelmaking in South Deering. The closing started a period of economic hard times on Chicago's Southeast Side, causing 3,500 employees to lose their jobs. The economic effects rippled throughout the community. Layoffs and closings occurred in other mills as well. It was as if the Southeast Side had been hit by a depression. This photograph was taken by Margaret Baughman in May 1982.

Frank Lumpkin, a 30-year employee, headed the Save Our Jobs Committee, made up of former Wisconsin Steel employees who sought to reopen part of the mill and win back-pay and other benefits. They filed suit against International Harvester seeking as much as $90 million in compensation. They settled the law suit in 1988 for $14.8 million. In 1989, the steelworkers filed suit against Environdyne Industries, the owner of the mill when it shut down. They won a smaller settlement in 1996. This photo was taken just before the building was demolished.

On April 10, 1992, United States Steel South Works, the largest mill on the Southeast Side, closed its doors forever. The employer of almost 18,000 at its peak had only 700 workers at South Works when it shut down. Pictured above is what was once the busiest steel mill in the area. A single railroad track winds through empty property. The building on the right is the electrical power sub station that provided power to the plant. To the left in the background are the smokestacks of the State Line Generating Station.

Southeast Side neighborhoods had numerous local organizations that created a strong sense of community. The Avalon Trails Improvement Association dealt with many problems including streets and alleys and environmental issues. It was instrumental in obtaining a new school, new field house, and new library. Pictured from left to right are Bernie Michalski, John Young, Judith Lihota, Edward Borowski, and Donna Young at the 25th Anniversary celebration in 1988.

On December 7, 1991, Chicago Public Library Commissioner John Duff cut the ribbon opening the new library in Hegewisch. It marked the successful conclusion of a campaign started in 1983 for a new library. Several community organizations were involved.

Several landfills are located on the Southeast Side. Pictured is the Paxton II landfill, opened in the early 1970s and closed in 1992. Despite numerous court battles, the landfill exceeded its permitted height by over 100 feet. In 1999, the 17-story tall, 58-acre landfill was in danger of collapse, and emergency procedures were taken to stabilize it and to avoid a "garbalanche."

A strong grass-roots environmental movement developed as the ecology of the region was damaged by heavy industry and by the large number of landfills in the area. Pictured are demonstrators protesting against a government plan to ship napalm through the Calumet region. They were successful in their efforts.

In 1990, the City of Chicago announced plans to build the Lake Calumet Airport. Almost all of Hegewisch and portions of South Deering and the East Side would have been eliminated to make room for the airport. Consequently, a huge anti-airport movement developed. Among the groups who protested the airport were the Hegewisch Airport Opponents, led by Virginia Cap. One of the many anti-airport protests is shown here. The airport was never built.

Eight

THE FUTURE

The future of Chicago's Southeast Side is still undetermined. Will industry redevelop the area still retaining many of the natural resources that made it so attractive to developers more than a century ago? Will economic development occur and revitalize the economy of the area? If development occurs, will it be friendly to the environment and to the ecosystem of the area? Will the area return to its historical role as a popular hunting and fishing destination? Will the area become a nature preserve where environmental restoration returns the ecology of the region to a more natural setting?

Nature and industry have been engaged in a monumental struggle to control the region since its beginning. The region was a popular hunting and fishing destination long before industrial development took place, and these activities continue to take place in the area. It is also still a very popular place for bird watchers to visit. The City of Chicago has proposed an Environmental Center for the area. Developers are looking at the available land, vacated by older, heavy industries, for future investment.

The picture above illustrates the stark contrasts that abound in the area. Duck hunters in the marshes of Chicago's Southeast Side enjoy nature while smoke pours out of the smokestacks of heavy industry in the background.

Fishing has been a popular past time for local residents and visitors to the area. Pictured in a photo entitled "Good Catch," a member of the Schupp family shows the results of his day fishing on the Calumet River in 1914.

The Southeast Sportsmen's Club, headquartered on the shores of Wolf Lake, has made use of the natural amenities of the region since its founding in 1938. Pictured is a pheasant release by club members. The pheasants had been raised at the club facilities.

This 1982 photo was taken by Sue Matczak for the Southeast Chicago Historical Project. The beach at Calumet Park sits very close to the State Line Generating Station. The picture shows the proximity of recreational and industrial uses of the land on the Southeast Side.

The Lake Calumet Study Committee was founded in 1980 to improve conditions in the Calumet region, which includes Chicago's Southeast Side. Among its numerous goals were preservation of Lake Calumet wetlands, opposition to any expansion of the waste disposal industry, and support for a Calumet Ecological Park. One of the groups that developed from this committee was the Calumet Ecological Park Association (CEPA). Pictured are members of CEPA at one of their first events, a tour of the area in August of 1993.

Lake Calumet Area Treasure Map

The Lake Calumet area is situated between the Illinois Heritage Corridor and the Indiana Dunes National Lakeshore. The map at right shows the proposed corridors which would make up the park lands. A detailed map (below) of the land surrounding Lake Calumet shows the wealth of natural resources threatened by inappropriate development and pollution. Only four of the sites shown on the map are protected areas.

Lake Calumet Treasures

Areas marked with an asterisk (*) are threatened. The size of each area indicated where known.

1   * **Altgeld Gardens Marsh**
   16 acres

2   **Beaubien Woods Forest Preserve**
   250 acres

3   * **Big Marsh**
   290 acres

4   * **Burnham Prairie (not shown on map)**
   175 acres

5   * **Calumet River**

6   * **Deadstick Pond**
   80 acres

7   * **Eggers Woods Extension**

8   **Eggers Woods Forest Preserve**
   250 acres

9   * **Grand Calumet River**

10   * **Hegewisch Marsh**
   140 acres

11   * **Heron Pond**
   50 acres

12   * **Hyde Lake**
   40 acres

Lake Calumet Treas
continued

13   * **Indian Ridge Mars**
   105 acres

14   * **Indian Ridge Mars**
   60 acres

15   * **Interchange Marsh**
   11.8 acres

16   * **Kensington Marsh**
   shown on map)
   15 acres (mitigation)

17   * **Lake Calumet**
   540 acres

18   * **Little Calumet Rive**

19   * **Migrant Bird Trap**
   shown on map)
   16 acres

20   * **O'Brien Lock Marsh**
   Whitford Pond
   120 acres

21   **Powderhorn Lake F**
   Preserve
   175 acres

22   * **Powderhorn Lake**
   Extension
   10 acres

23   * **Railroad Prairie**
   190 acres

24   * **Turning Basin Wetl**

25   * **Van Vlissingen Prai**
   160 acres

26   **William W. Powers**
   tion Area (Wolf Lake
   613 acres

Map Legend

— boundaries of lakes, rivers

---- streets, roads, expressways

· · · · · boundaries of parks, forest preserves

♦ roadside parking spc

+++++ railroad

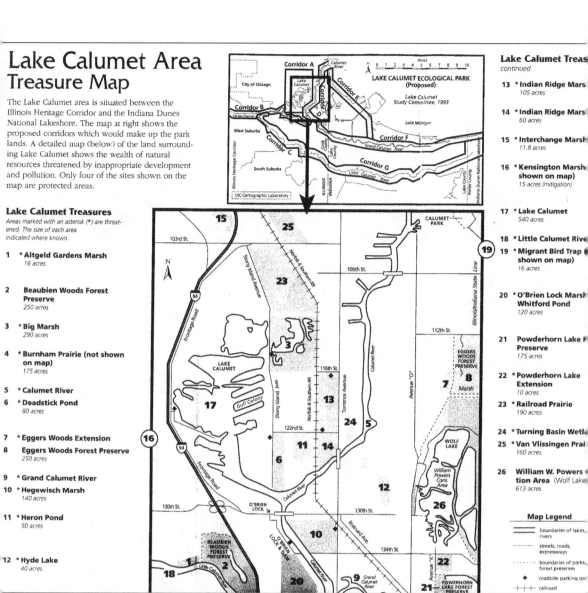

CEPA developed a map in 1993 showing natural areas in the Lake Calumet region, most of which were unprotected. The smaller map shows aspects of the proposal for the Ecological Park made by the Lake Calumet Study Committee. A National Park Service study in 1998 recognized the national significance of the region and suggested pursuing a National Heritage Area designation. To date no legislation has been introduced in Congress.

Pictured is a view of the "Bush" and Saint Michael's Church from the vacant United States Steel property. Once covered with steel-making facilities and railroad tracks, the 576 acres have been for sale since 1997. Solo Cup Corporation has agreed to purchase 118 acres for a new plant that will employ 1,000 workers, 450 of them in new jobs. Over 100 acres will be conveyed to the city for a park and other amenities. The balance of the acreage is still up for sale.

At first glance, one might wonder if this photo is symbolic of the sunset or sunrise of Chicago's Southeast Side. It is, in fact, a sunrise at Wolf Lake and perhaps a sign of better times for this highly interesting community.

ACKNOWLEDGMENTS

This book is dedicated to the current and former residents of Chicago's Southeast Side who have donated historical materials to the Southeast Historical Project and to the Southeast Historical Museum and provided the stories which resulted in this book.

The book would not have been possible without the work done by the Southeast Chicago Historical Project, which began the process of collecting and organizing materials which helped to tell the story of Chicago's Southeast Side. Local historians James P. Fitzgibbons and Ed Sadlowski worked with Columbia College Project Director James R. Martin, Associate Director Dominic A. Pacyga, Columbia College staff and students, and area residents in the project. The Southeast Chicago Historical Project was funded by Columbia College, the National Endowment for the Humanities, and the Illinois Humanities Council. The materials collected by the Project are part of the collection of the Southeast Historical Museum located in the Calumet Park Field House on Chicago's Southeast Side. The collection and the Museum continue to grow. Thanks to the Project and to all the many residents of the area who helped with the Project.

I would like to thank the following individuals and institutions for their guidance, advice, and assistance in preparing this second book on Chicago's Southeast Side: Dominic Pacyga, a friend and mentor who introduced me to the opportunity of co-authoring *Chicago's Southeast Side*, which has led to a second book about the area; the Southeast Historical Society and the James Fitzgibbons Historical Museum, especially Ora Coon, Barney Janecki, Joe Mulac, Alex Savastano, and Frank Stanley; Marian Byrnes, Judy Lihota, and Virginia Cap for their insights into the environmental movement on the Southeast Side; Mike, Debbie, and Helen Aniol for their expertise on the Hegewisch community; and Rosemarie Kruse for her assistance.

Thanks to the following who assisted by providing photographs or other materials used in the book: Raymond Mulac for the use of his wonderful post card collection, Judy Lihota, Mike Boos, Linda Moll, the Olejnik family, Dr. James E. Landing, Keith Ryder, David Holmberg, Nancy Margraff, Joe Bastie, Jim Rossi, Frank and Bea Lumpkin, the Calumet Ecological Park Association, and the East Side Chamber of Commerce.

Most of all I want to thank my dear wife, Kathy, for her patience and understanding during the period when I worked on this book. Without her support the book would not have been possible.

A portion of the royalties from this book will benefit the Southeast Historical Society and Museum.

Visit us at
arcadiapublishing.com

CPSIA information can be obtained
at www.ICGtesting.com
Printed in the USA
LVHW061601220323
742296LV00006B/433

9 781531 613068